Antarctic Antics

A BOOK OF PENGUIN P

WRITTEN BY

Judy Sierra

ILLUSTRATED BY

Jose Aruego
& Ariane Dewey

Voyager Books • Harcourt, Inc.

San Diego   New York   London

T0116024

www.hmhco.com

First Voyager Books edition 2003
Voyager Books is a trademark of Harcourt, Inc., registered in the United States of
America and/or other jurisdictions.

The Library of Congress has cataloged the hardcover edition as follows:
Sierra, Judy.
Antarctic antics: a book of penguin poems/by Judy Sierra; illustrated by Jose Aruego
and Ariane Dewey.
p.   cm.
Summary: A collection of poems celebrating the habits and habitat of emperor penguins.
1. Penguins—Juvenile poetry.   2. Antarctic regions—Juvenile poetry.
3. Children's poetry, American.   [1. Penguins—Poetry.   2. Antarctic regions—Poetry.
3. American poetry.]   I. Aruego, Jose, ill.
II. Dewey, Ariane, ill.   III. Title.
PS3569.I39A53   1998
811'.54—dc20   96-41041
ISBN 0-15-201006-8
ISBN 0-15-204602-X pb

MER

4500828555

The illustrations in this book were made with pen and ink, gouache, watercolor,
and pastel on Strathmore Kit paper.
The display type was set in Worcester Round.
The text type was set in Golden Type.
Color separations by Bright Arts, Ltd., Singapore
Printed and bound by RR Donnelley, China
Production supervision by Sandra Grebenar and Wendi Taylor
Designed by Lydia D'moch

The poems in this book are based on the real lives
and habits of emperor penguins. To find out more
about these fascinating flightless birds, see:

BOOKS

Barrett, Norman S. *Penguins.* New York: Franklin Watts,
   1991.
Patent, Dorothy Hinshaw. *Looking at Penguins.* New York:
   Holiday House, 1993.
Wexo, John B. *Penguins.* Mankato, Minn.: Creative
   Education, Inc., 1989.

VIDEO

"Emperors of Antarctica." Discovery Channel Video Library.
   Discovery Communications, Inc., 1994.

For Liz Van Doren
—J. S.

For Juan
—J. A. & A. D.

A Hatchling's Song

I'm almost hatched!
I'm almost hatched!
I'm small, I'm wet,
I'm not out yet.
I'm almost hatched!

I'm pecking hard,
I'm pecking hard.
I'm tired, I'm weak,
It hurts my beak.
I'm pecking hard.

My head's outside,
My head's outside.
The moon is bright—
The world's so white!
My head's outside.

I'm really hatched,
I'm really hatched.
At last I'm free.
Hey, Dad, it's me!
I'm really hatched.

Mother Penguin's Vacation

Two months out at sea
Is a penguin's great thrill.
Each evening my dinner
Floats right into my bill.
Oh, I might make a meal
Of a slithery eel,
Or a cod, or a squid.
(*Gulp!* I think I just did—
I feel a long tentacle
Tickling my ventricle.)

Several shrimp swimming south
Are approaching my mouth—
So I'll just open wide
And invite them inside.
Yes, two months' vacation
Is a penguinish wish.
I've got nothing to do
But slurp squadrons of fish.
I'll grow gorgeously fat,
Then swim home in July,
To sing my new baby
A deep-sea lullaby.

My Father's Feet

To keep myself up off the ice,
I find my father's feet are nice.
I snuggle in his belly fluff,
And that's how I stay warm enough.

But when my father takes a walk,
My cozy world begins to rock.
He shuffles left, I hold on tight.

Oh no! He's wobbling to the right.
Not left again! Oops, here he goes.

Do you suppose my father knows
I'm hanging on to his warm toes?

Regurgitate

It's been one whole hour since I ate.
Why is my dinner always late?
While you and Mom procrastinate,
I might become a featherweight.
You know what I'd appreciate?
Cough it up, Dad! Regurgitate!

I Am Looking for My Mother

I am looking for my mother.
But you all look like each other.
So I'll do what Mama said,
And I'll use my ears instead.

AWK

EEK

ECK   ICK

ECK!
My mom does not say *eck*.
She might give me a peck
On the back of my neck,
But she'd never say *eck*.

ICK!
My mom wouldn't say *ick*!
She would call me her chick
As she gives me a lick,
But she *couldn't* say *ick*.

EEK!
My mom does not say *eek*.
She might let out a shriek
That would make the ice creak,
But she'd never squeak *eek*.

ACK

AWK!
What mom would say *awk*?
Awk is only a squawk,
And it's no way to talk.
Go away with your *awk*!

ACK? ACK, ACK?
Such a sweet sounding *ack*.
Lovely Mom, you've come back.
Did you bring me a snack?
Only *my* mom says *ack*.

Penguins' First Swim

Ten little penguins all in a line—
One jumps in, and now there are nine.
Nine little penguins, how they hesitate—
One tumbles in, and now there are eight.

Eight little penguins pushin' and shovin'—
One slides in, and now there are seven.
Seven little penguins, scarcely more than chicks—
One slips in, and now there are six.

Six little penguins can't decide to dive—
One falls in, and now there are five.
Five little penguins huddle on the shore—
One flops in, and now there are four.

Four little penguins fidget fearfully—
One hops in, and now there are three.
Three little penguins wonder what to do—
One rolls in, and now there are two. . . .

Two little penguins missing all the fun—
They both leap in, and now there are . . .
Ten little penguins, brave as they can be,
Splashing in the waves of the salty southern sea.

Predator Riddles

What's black and white
And mean all over?
A mighty swimmer,
A restless rover.
He looks like a fish
From head to tail.
But he isn't a fish;
He's a _____.

KILLER WHALE

The gray of the sea
Hides the gray of her fur,
As she waits in the waves
For a penguin to stir.
But she isn't our friend—
No, she's waiting to steal
One of us for her supper.
She's a cruel _____.

LEOPARD SEAL

He's a two-legged pest.
He's revolting and rude,
Stealing eggs from our nests,
Chasing chicks, snatching food.

But can you believe this?
Though it does seem absurd,
This creature's our cousin.
He's a skulking _____.

SKUA BIRD

Diary of a Very Short Winter Day

At the first hint of dawn
I awake with a yawn
And follow my cousins
(All thirty-three dozen)
To the end of the land,
Where we stand and we stand,
Playing who'll-dive-in-first,
And, fearing the worst,
We listen for seals
Who want us for meals.
I see one penguin lunge,
Then in we all plunge,
Take a bath, gulp a snack,
And climb out in a pack. . . .

Hurry back to our home
For a quick preen and comb
So our feathers aren't wet
As we watch the sun set.

Belly Sliding

Our forepenguins settled here
Twenty million years ago.
They grew blubber for the cold;
They grew feathers for the snow.
They grew weary of the dark
Winter nights that last all day.
They decided even penguins
Have to take the time to play.
So we go belly sliding,
Ta-tum-tum-tummy gliding;

Down the glacier's glassy side,
We begin our ripping ride.
And soon we're stomach slipping,
Fearlessly flip-flop-flipping,
Flying sixty miles an hour
Solely fueled by penguin power.
Soaring far too fast to stop,
We shoot off the glacier's top;
Downward through the air we drop,
Landing with a wet *ker-plop*.
Tumble out and, with a grin,
Shout, "Let's do it all again!"

Be My Penguin

Be my penguin,
My *sweet* penguin.
I fancy your feathers so smooth and so sleek,
The way snowflakes dance on the down of your cheek.
The curve of your beak makes my flippers grow weak.
Be my penguin.

We'll ramble romantically by the sea;
My siblings will sing you a symphony;
I'll catch you an anchovy. Darling, why can't you be
My sweet penguin?

At night, by the light of the southern aurora,
We'll navigate northward toward Bora Bora
While you eat the fauna and I eat the flora.
Be my penguin.

I'll carve you a castle inside an ice floe,
A cave where the chilly winds never will blow.
Oh, how could you say no? Is your heart made of snow?
. . . Guess I'll just have to go find another penguin.

Be my penguin!
My *sweet* penguin!
I fancy your feathers so smooth and so sleek,
The way snowflakes dance on the down of your cheek.
The curve of your beak makes my flippers grow weak.
Oh please, be my penguin.

Antarctic Anthem

At the bottom of the planet
Lies a land of ice and granite:
Ant · arc · ti · ca! Ant · arc · ti · ca!
Where winter days are dark-tica.
It's the continent of our birth;
It's the coldest place on earth:
Ant · arc · ti · ca! Ant · arc · ti · ca!
You'd better wear your park-tica,
Or the brutal, blasting blizzards
Will freeze your beaks and gizzards.
Ant · arc · ti · ca! Ant · arc · ti · ca!

Come visit on a lark-tica!
We'll snuggle in the snow
When it's thirty-five below.
Ant·arc·ti·ca! Ant·arc·ti·ca!
It's grander than New York-tica.
Skyscraping icebergs roam
All across the frosty foam
In our sweet Antarctic home.